DISCOVERING WOLVES
A Nature Activity Book

By
Nancy Field
Corliss Karasov
Illustrated by Cary Hunkel

Produced in cooperation with the Timber Wolf Alliance

Text copyright © 1991 Dog-Eared Publications
Artwork copyright © 1991 Cary Hunkel
Second Printing 1992

ISBN 0-941042-10-3

Have You Ever Wondered?

It's a cool summer morning in the north. Four wolf pups are playing at their den under the watchful eye of their older brother. One pup playfully pulls at the pupsitter's tail while the others explore their new world. The rest of the pack is returning from a hunt.

Meanwhile, a group of wolf biologists is flying around the area in a plane. The biologists listen to their headphones for a soft beeping sound. Last spring they placed a radio collar around one wolf's neck. Now, beeping signals from the collar lead them to the pack.

The biologists spot five adult wolves just as they reach the den. They watch as pack members greet each other with nose rubbing, licking, and sniffing. The adults feed the pups deer meat that they have carried in their stomachs.

They are pleased to see the wolves are doing well with four pups. Perhaps wolves will survive in this area. The biologists fly on looking for signs of other packs and den sites. Another day they will return on foot to search for tracks. They will even howl to see if the wolves will answer.

While most of us will never see wolves in the wild, we can enjoy learning their secrets. We can visit parks and forests and hear biologists tell about the place wolves have as predators in the world. We can learn how they radio collar and track wolves. Use your Discovery Book to learn more about these magnificent animals.

2

3

Meet Great, Great...Grandad: The Wolf

It's no accident that many dogs you know look like wolves. Wolves are the ancestors to all dogs, from poodles to Saint Bernards. Along with foxes and coyotes, they all belong to the family *Canidae*.

Reading about wolves can help us understand dogs. Dogs inherited their body and behavior traits from wolves. For example, the hunting behaviors you see in some dogs help wolves survive in the wild.

Yet we should not forget that dogs have important differences from Great Grandad. For hundreds of years, dogs have been bred to obey humans. Wolves are still wild animals. They cannot be trained to be obedient, family pets.

Now meet the two **species**, or kinds, of wolf: the red wolf and the gray wolf. Color the wolves.

How are wolves and dogs alike?

The Red Wolf
(Scientific Name *Canis rufus*)

The least-known wolf is a small wolf from southeastern United States.

The red wolf is about the size of a collie. It is 4 to 5 1/2 feet long (1.3 m) and weighs from 40 to 80 pounds (34 kg). Color its back reddish brown. Color the belly and underparts buffy white to pinkish.

4

The Gray Wolf
(Scientific Name *Canis lupus*)

Most wolves we read about are gray wolves. These wolves go by different names depending on where they live. The gray wolves that live among the trees in the Eastern parts of the United States and Canada are known as timber wolves. Arctic wolves, Mexican wolves, Texas gray wolves, and northern Rocky Mountain wolves are also gray wolves.

Few animals live in as many places as gray wolves do. They live everywhere from deserts to the frozen arctic regions.

Not all gray wolves look alike...not all gray wolves are gray! A wolf living in the desert looks different from one in a northern woods. How might their colors help each wolf survive in the wild?

The smallest wolves live in the Arabian desert (about 37 pounds, 17 kg). They tend to be light-colored and have big ears. Color this one tan.

The largest wolves are found in the cold, far north (100 to 120 or more pounds or 54 kg). Many are white. Thick toe pads protect their feet. Leave this one white.

Mid-sized wolves live in milder climates (55 to 100 pounds, 45 kg). They measure 5 to 6 feet from nose to tail tip. Their colors range from white to black. Often they are light gray or brown sprinkled with black, white, and yellow. The underparts and legs are off-white. Color one white, one black, and one gray.

Disappearing Wolves

Yesterday

Hundreds of years ago, the wolf was the most widespread land mammal, other than the human. The wolf's **range**, or area where it lived, covered North America, Europe, and Asia. About the only places wolves did not live were in the driest of deserts and in wet tropical forests.

Today

Today, wolves are gone from much of the globe.

Who's Missing?

Notice the little numbers on each wolf. To see which wolves have disappeared, take a black crayon or pencil and **cross out the following wolves:**

North America: wolves 40 - 69
Europe: wolves 84 - 94
Asia: wolves 147 - 157

Wolves no longer live in the areas you crossed off.

Who's Left?

The wolves remaining on your map show where wolves can still be found. But they don't show how many wolves can be found in each region. Numbers of wolves in some areas are low. They are **endangered** or **threatened**. These wolves need protection in order to survive.

Gray Wolf

Red Wolf

Extinct animals once lived on Earth but have vanished. They are gone forever.

Endangered animals are alive today but face extinction in all or large parts of their range.

Threatened animals are those likely to become endangered in the near future.

Game animals can be hunted.

6

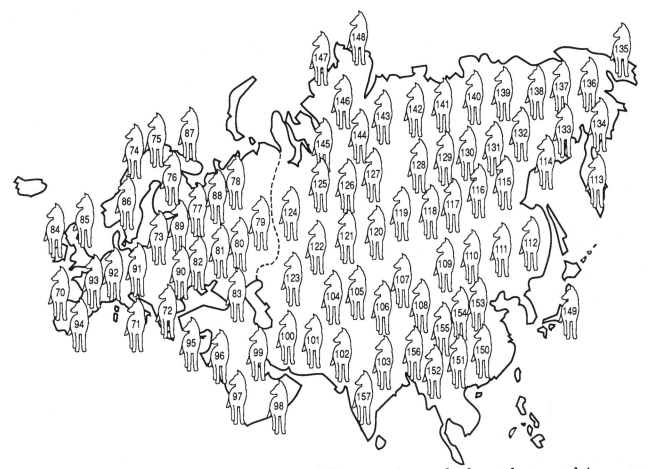

Discover where wolves are in danger of disappearing and where they are doing well. **Use three colored crayons to circle the following regions:**

Region	Circle In	Wolves Here Are	Number of Wolves 1600*	1960	1990
Alaska	Green	Game animal	about 10,000	about 10,000	about 5-7,000
Idaho	Red	Endangered	about 8,000	0	fewer than 15
Michigan	Red	Endangered	about 8,000	about 50	about 24
Minnesota	Orange	Threatened	about 8,000	350 - 700	about 1750
Montana	Red	Endangered	about 10,000	0	about 40
Washington	Red	Endangered	about 6,000	0	fewer than 10
Wisconsin	Red	Endangered	about 6,000	0	about 35
Wyoming	Red	Endangered	about 9,000	0	0
Other States	Red	Endangered	uncertain	about 50	0

Canada	Green	Game animal	about 95,000	about 50,000	about 58,000
Mexico	Red	Endangered	uncertain	uncertain	fewer than 10
Europe	**	**	uncertain	uncertain	uncertain
Asia	**	**	uncertain	uncertain	uncertain

*Numbers for 1600 are an estimate.

**Wolf survival in Europe and Asia varies from country to country. Wolves once roamed throughout Europe. Now they are doing well in only a few wilderness areas in Poland, Spain, Portugal, and Italy. Many wolves live in China and the Soviet Union.

Why do you think wolves are increasing in some places? Keep reading to find out.

Why Did Wolves Disappear?

After thousands of years sharing the earth with humans, why did wolves suddenly vanish from many corners of the world?

During the past two centuries, more and more people have spread out across the world. They compete with animals for food and living space. Less wild space means fewer wolves.

People's hate and fear of wolves increased. This led many humans to try to rid the world of wolves. Laws were passed that encouraged people to kill large numbers of wolves throughout America, Europe, and Asia.

Below are six ways wolves disappeared. One is labelled. Can you label the other five? Circle those that are still threats today.

A. BOUNTY HUNTERS

B. _____

C. _____

D. _____

E. _____

F. _____

Answers on last page

But human attitudes are changing today. We are learning to respect wolves. Laws now protect wolves in many regions of the world.

Yet, wolves still have problems. Wolves need especially large, wild areas with plenty of food. Today, loss of living space, or **habitat**, is one of the biggest problems. Habitats are important places. These homes provide food, water, shelter, and space for living creatures.

Woeful Wolf Tales

Nature's Hunters

Wolves were probably most misunderstood because they are **predators**. Predators are animals that hunt and feed on other animals, called **prey**.

People are beginning to understand that predators have an important place in the world. They are part of nature's balancing act. The picture below shows how predators and prey balance each other.

When Predators Aren't Around

Deer herds can grow and grow and grow.

Only bad weather and disease will slow down herd growth.

Huge deer herds overeat their food.

As their food disappears, the whole herd begins to starve.

Links in Food Chain

It is natural for one thing to eat another. It starts when green plants get energy from the sun.

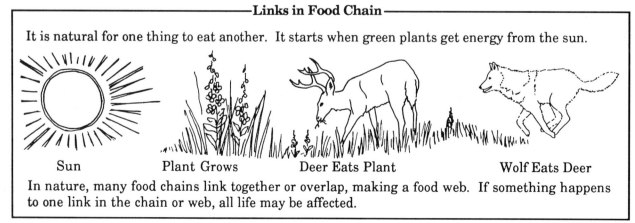

Sun   Plant Grows   Deer Eats Plant   Wolf Eats Deer

In nature, many food chains link together or overlap, making a food web. If something happens to one link in the chain or web, all life may be affected.

When Predators Are Around

Are Predators Cruel and Wicked?

A wolf eating a deer is no different than a human cutting into a steak. Both are predators. Neither is "mean or bad." They eat to live.

By killing some deer, wolves help keep the deer herd smaller. Smaller herds have more food.

When the number of deer is low, wolves have fewer pups and may also starve. In this way the deer control the number of wolves.

Hunters can sometimes replace wolves and control deer numbers.

Isle Royale

Isle Royale is a large, wilderness island in Lake Superior. Scientists in this national park have been studying predators and prey for long time. Wolves are the predators. Moose and beaver are the prey.

Wolf biologists have found that wolves tend to catch and kill the easiest prey. These are often very old, young, sick, injured, or weak moose. Wolves will also try to kill strong animals, but strong moose can outrun them, fight them off, or injure them. Fewer moose also means more food for the rest of the herd.

Designed for Predation

Wolves are beautifully suited for hunting. Look closely for clues to why wolves can track, chase, and kill an 800-pound moose–yet they can't survive by eating plants as deer do.

Ears A wolf has a keen sense of hearing. It can hear sounds up to six miles away (9.7 km). It can also hear some high-pitched sounds we can't hear.

Eyes A wolf has sharp eyesight. This helps it find and follow prey.

Nose A wolf's sense of smell is about 100 times better than ours. It can smell prey a mile (1.6 km) or more away if the wind is right.

Teeth and Jaws The teeth and jaws are made to eat meat. As weapons, the wolf uses its 42 teeth when attacking, killing, and eating prey. Powerful jaws help crush bones.

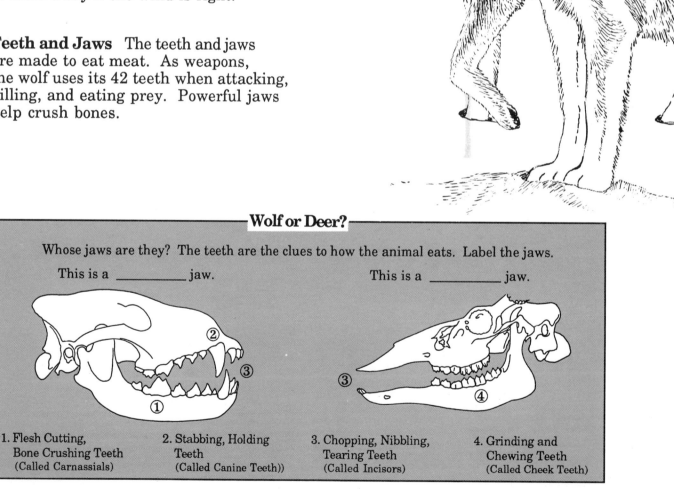

Wolf or Deer?

Whose jaws are they? The teeth are the clues to how the animal eats. Label the jaws.

This is a _____ jaw.   This is a _____ jaw.

1. Flesh Cutting, Bone Crushing Teeth (Called Carnassials)
2. Stabbing, Holding Teeth (Called Canine Teeth))
3. Chopping, Nibbling, Tearing Teeth (Called Incisors)
4. Grinding and Chewing Teeth (Called Cheek Teeth)

Live in Packs There is strength in numbers. Meat-eaters that hunt in packs are more successful in making a kill. By working as a team, wolves are able to bring down prey much larger than themselves.

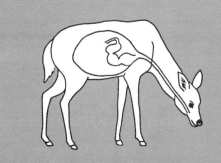

Fur The wolf has a double coat. Long guard hairs on top work like an umbrella. They shed moisture to keep the wolf dry. Dense, wooly underfur keeps the wolf warm. The wolf sheds its underfur in the summer.

Tail In winter, a wolf can curl its thick, furred tail around its face. This way the nose is protected down to - 60° F (- 51° C). In summer, the tail helps keep insects off the face.

Legs Speed and endurance help a wolf catch dinner. The faster the predator, the more successful its hunting. Long, powerful legs help the wolf chase prey for 20 miles (32 km) or more. A wolf can run from 24 to 40 miles per hour (38 to 64 km per hour).

Feet Feet are designed for running. The front foot is slightly larger than the rear. Paws spread slightly when they hit the ground, acting like snowshoes on snow and ice.

They can't eat each other's food.

Plant-eater stomach The deer has a complex, four-part stomach. Special bacteria digest plants.

Meat-eater stomach The wolf has a simple stomach. Extra acids assist in the slow process of breaking down meat.

Family Album

Meet the Moose Lake Pack, a real wolf **pack**, or family group, in northern Wisconsin. Wolf biologists have been studying this pack since 1980. Like most wolf packs, this one is a close-knit family. They have a Mom and Dad, their pups, youngsters, and adult offspring. They eat, sleep, travel, hunt, and play together.

Mom and Dad, also called the **alpha pair**, lead the pack. Wolf packs have a well organized leadership order. This way each wolf knows who's boss, or **dominant**, and who's the follower, or **subordinate**. Understanding this helps wolves work together without serious fights.

THE ALPHA PAIR

Here are Mom and Dad, our alpha pair. They are letting everyone know that they are in charge by holding their tails up and ears erect. They make all group decisions such as when to hunt and where to sleep. Usually they are the only animals to mate. (The word "*alpha*" is the first letter in the Greek alphabet.)

BETA MALE

Beta male lowers his head and tail when around the alpha pair to let them know he will obey them. (The word "*beta*" is the second letter in the Greek alphabet.)

THE YEARLINGS

Our yearlings are low ranking members of the pack. Their job is to fine tune wolf skills so they will be able to take care of themselves. Scientists can often recognize each wolf by color patterns on the face and fur.

THE PUPS

Mom dug this den to shelter the pups. Other pack members bring food to her. She nurses the pups, but the whole pack will share in feeding and caring for them when they are out of the den.

14

SCAPEGOAT

The lowest ranking member of the pack is called the **scapegoat**. This wolf shows its submission by keeping its fur and ears flattened, its body close to the ground, and its tail often tucked between its legs.

OUR DISPERSER

This is the last our family saw of the disperser. This young adult left the pack and became a **lone wolf**. It may find a new, suitable place to live and a mate.

Leadership Order or **Dominance Hierarchy**

Place these wolves on the ladder in order from top to bottom wolf:

Beta Male
Alpha Male
Alpha Female
Scapegoat
Yearlings

Pup Stuff

Born—spring
Number of pups—often 4 to 6
Can smell—first day
Can hear—few days
Deaf and blind—at birth
Eyes open—11 to 15 days
Baby teeth—2 weeks
Out of den—3 to 4 weeks
Begin to hunt—autumn
Full grown—one year
Able to mate—22 months

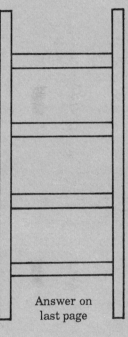

Answer on last page

FAMILY PUP CARE

A pup is nuzzling an adult for food. Adults eat food and carry it in their stomachs to the pups. The pups nuzzle the adult's mouth, causing it to regurgitate or *"throw up"* the partly digested food for the pups to eat.

PUP SITTING

Beta male is pup-sitting at a **rendezvous site**, or camp. The pups are not strong enough to hunt until fall. They are working out a small social order of their own.

School Time

The first summer of a pup's life is important. A pup has to learn many lessons on how to live within the pack. Survival depends on knowing wolf pack rules.

Help this pup through kindergarten. You must stop at each learning station without crossing or retracing your own path.

Become friends with other pack members. The bonds will help keep the pack together.

Learn to obey pack leaders.

Test strengths and weaknesses of litter-mates. Discover who is top pup.

Learn hunting skills from parents.

Learn your place in the pack.

Strengthen muscles. Develop coordination.

Learn behaviors to avoid hurting each other.

Graduation Certificate

You have learned your lessons and are a working member of the team.

How Do Wolves Say Hello?

Have you seen dogs jump up to greet their owners, bark at strangers, or roll over when another dog approaches? Then you already know something about how wolves communicate. Dogs inherited most of their language from their ancestors, the wolves.

Wolves use three different languages:

       1. **Sound—Howls, Barks, Whimpers, and Growls**
       2. **Special Scents—Including Scent Marking**
       3. **Body Language—Body Positions and Movements**

See if you can identify the body language or signal each wolf is using by **matching each wolf with its message below**. Look closely at the face, ears, tail, and body. Each message can be used more than once.

MESSAGES

Hello!

Let's play

I won't fight ...I'll obey

I'm the leader

This is my territory

Stay away...

Answers on last page

Calls of the Wild

Deep in the woods, one wolf leans its head back and begins to howl. Moments later, six distant wolves join the singing. Each sings its own tune. Together, they sound like a dozen wolves.

Later, the wolves get together. They bark, whimper, and growl at each other. What are they saying? Do they talk for enjoyment? We don't know for sure.

Wolves use sound along with body language to communicate. Howling and occasional barking are used to talk over great distances. Barks, growls, and whimpers are used when wolves are close together.

Wolf Sounds
Choose from these sounds to answer questions below. Practice the sounds.

Howling—songs of ow-oo-ow, yi-e-e-e, and arr-rrr-rrr-oo-ooo

Barking—yip, yap, huff, wuff, woof

Whimpering—whine, squeak, and squeal

Growling—snarl, grr-rr-rr

Do Wolves Howl at the Moon?

No. People may hear more wolves on moonlit nights because we are more likely to be outside then. Wolves howl both night and day.

What sound would a wolf make if it wanted to:

- call to far-away pack members

- ask its mother for food or attention

- tell another wolf to stay away from its food

- tell neighboring wolves to stay off its land

- tell the leader "I won't fight!"

- tell wolf pups to follow

- tell other pack members to follow

- tell others it is alarmed

_____

_____

_____

_____

_____

_____

_____

_____

Answers on last page

Wolf Talk

Animals that live in packs must be great at talking, or **communicating**—just to get along with each other. Wolf language is beautiful to watch and hear. When wolf pack members are together, they constantly touch, sniff, and make noises and body signals to each other. **By "talking" with each other they can do the following:**

1. Keep the Pack Together	**2. Work as a Team**

Ears up, tail high mean "I'm boss!"

Ears down, tail down mean "I'll obey."

3. Avoid Fights and Communicate Rights

4. Mark and Protect Territory

Draw a simple picture for each box. Remember to show tails, ears, and other body language. A sample is done for you. **Find another person or team of people to help get ideas. Or can you create a short story, play, or sound video using these situations?**

Ideas on answer page

19

Keep Off My Property!

Have you ever seen a dog urinating on rocks, dirt piles, and trees around its yard? It's leaving **scent posts,** or messages, marking the boundaries of its yard. Wolves leave fresh scent posts around their land every few weeks to claim ownership. Scent posts are like "keep off my property" signs for other wolves.

A wolf pack often has an extremely large yard, or **territory**. This is the area the pack will defend against other wolf packs. With a territory, they spend less time and energy fighting other packs. They have more time to raise young and hunt for food. When deer or moose are spread out over large areas, wolves need larger territories.

Territories can change in shape and size depending on the season. Wolves in the far north follow migrating caribou, so they don't have a year-round territory. Sometimes territories overlap.

The map below shows territories of two wolf packs: Pack A and Pack B. **Find the territories by connecting the scent posts numbered 1 to 10 for each pack.**

Symbols for scent posts: Pack A = ○   Pack B = △

Give each pack a name and write this name inside its territory.

The size of a territory ranges from 50 to 150 or more square miles. One city in the Midwest covers an area of about five square miles. About 20,000 people live in this city. Using the square to the right, about how many cities this size would fit in Pack B's territory? _____ How big is territory B? _____ This is an average size territory. How big is your city or a city near you? How many cities that size would fit in Pack B's territory? _____

A City 5 square miles

Is there room between packs for a lone wolf? Color the lone wolf's space.

Answer on last page

Wolf Survival Game

Can you survive for one season as a wolf?

Survival is not easy for wolves. They need to be more than just good hunters to survive. They need good health, good social skills, and luck. Many wolves die from disease, starvation, hunting, poisoning, and more. Usually, only half of all pups survive their first year.

You will need:

- Playing piece for each player. You can use small objects like coins or pebbles. Make sure each player's marker looks different. Or you may trace the markers below. Color and cut them out.

- A die (one of a pair of dice). Or find six objects, such as paper pieces or pebbles. Number them 1, 2, 3, 4, 5, and 6. Place them in a container like a paper bag or hat.

Directions:

1. Your goal is to survive one season as a wolf. Collect 500 food points to live. More than one wolf can win.
2. One to six people can play. Each player is a pack member and shares food points when a moose or deer is killed. There must be at least 2 players to kill an adult moose.
3. When it is your turn, throw the die or draw a number. Move the correct number of spaces. Follow the instructions on the board.
4. Keep track of the food points you collect. When you land on a deer or moose, share the points between the players, except anyone on the Lone Wolf Trail. If the points do not divide evenly, keep the extra points for yourself.
5. Lone wolves on the Lone Wolf Trail cannot catch healthy moose or deer. They can only get young or sick deer. Lone wolves do not share or receive points from other players.
6. Playing alone you cannot catch healthy moose or deer. You can only get young or sick deer.
7. If one pack wolf finishes first, that wolf continues to get shared points from other wolves on the trail.

Your Food: You eat moose, deer, beaver, snowshoe hare, and occasionally squirrels and mice.

Moose	Deer	Beaver	Snowshoe Hare	Squirrel	30 Mice *(Wolf Candy Bars)*

Wolf Survival Game

1 point

Killed by car on new highway. Start over as new wolf.

Start

20 points

Missed Deer. Lose 5 points.

Old deer. Share 80 points.

Fight with other pack members. Lose 10 points.

Poisoned! Killed! Start over as new wolf.

Share 400 points.

Fat deer. Share 100 points.

Catch young deer. 40 points

Catch sick deer. 60 points

Finish

Weak from malnutrition. Lose 50 points.

20 points

1 point

Catch sick deer. 60 points

1 point

20 points

Catch young deer. 40 points

Injured leg: Another wolf brings food. 10 points

Missed Deer. Lose 5 points.

Fight with lead wolf. Leave pack and follow the **Lone Wolf Trail.**

Shot by poacher. You're out of the game.

Extreme cold kills many deer. Eat dead, starved deer. 60 points.

Catch young deer. 40 points

2 points

Catch young deer. 40 points

1 point

Weakened by Lyme Disease. Lose 200 points.

Catch sick deer. 60 points

Catch sick deer. 60 points

Catch young deer. 40 points

Catch sick deer. 60 points

Weak from tapeworm. Lose 50 points.

Catch young deer. 40 points

Catch young deer. 40 points

Couldn't catch moose. Lose 10 points

Share 90 points.

Kicked by deer! Broken ribs! Lose 50 points.

Missed moose. Lose 10 points.

Attacked by injured bear. Lose 5 points.

Catch young deer. 40 points

Share 100 points.

Porcupine quill in mouth gets infected. Lose 20 points.

Catch sick deer. 60 points

Share 400 points.

20 points

Catch sick deer. 60 points

Share 400 points.

If you land **Detour** on this spot

2 points

1 point

Catch sick deer. 60 points

Ravens lead wolves to deer kill. Share 100 points.

Share 100 points.

Detour to logged area. Great deer habitat.

2 points

Catch sick deer. 60 points

Couldn't catch moose. Lose 10 points

Catch sick deer. 60 points

Share 400 points.

Catch young deer. 40 points

2 points

Sick deer. Share 80 points.

Missed deer. Lose 5 points.

Share 90 points.

Share 400 points.

Couldn't catch moose. Lose 5 points.

Share 100 points.

20 points

2 points

What's for Dinner?

Does a wolf in Alaska have the same menu as a wolf in Minnesota? No! What a wolf eats depends on where it lives and the season of the year. Wolves usually live where they can find at least two or more kinds of prey. They mainly eat large hoofed animals. At times they eat small animals.

Travel around North America to discover what wolves eat. The map shows only one of the prey wolves eat in each area. **Unscramble the name of the prey at each stop.**

Most animals have several ways to protect themselves from predators. Only one defense is shown for each kind of animal pictured.

When you have unscrambled the animals, match them with the list of defenses below. Write the letter next to the animal's name.

Defenses of Prey Animals

A. Run swiftly

B. Kick

C. Use death-dealing hoofs

D. Escape up cliffs

E. Attack with antlers

F. Fly away

G. Blend with surroundings (hidden by camouflage)

H. Form defensive circle

I. Give warning to others

J. Run into open water

K. Gouge or hook with horns

L. Escape to a safe place

Remember, this isn't the only defense each animal could use. For example, the bighorn sheep could gouge with horns, escape up cliffs, or use hoofs.

1. Dlal hespe

_____

12. gbiohrn epehs

_____

11. rbveera

_____

10. kel

_____

Answers on last page

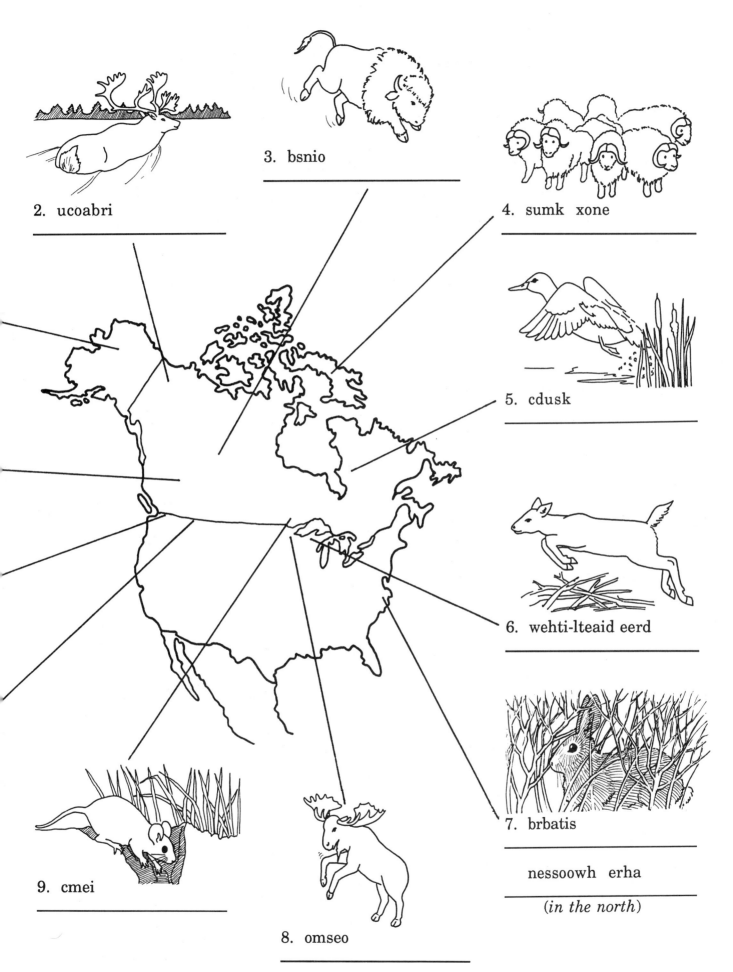

2. ucoabri

_____

3. bsnio

_____

4. sumk xone

_____

5. cdusk

_____

6. wehti-lteaid eerd

_____

7. brbatis

_____

nessoowh erha

_____
(*in the north*)

9. cmei

_____

8. omseo

_____

Deer Math

Hunters wonder if wolves could kill so many deer that there would not be enough left to provide food for their families. Should the deer hunters worry? You can help answer the question. **Solve the following math problem:**

One year, northern Wisconsin had 300,000 deer. About 50 wolves lived there.

Winter Season   Each wolf needed to eat one deer each 18 days or five deer for the season.

Deer at start of season	300,000
Deer accidentally killed by cars and other vehicles	- 3,500
Deer that died from starvation and other diseases	- 30,000
Fifty wolves ate	_____ deer
At the end of the season there were	_____ deer

Spring and Summer Seasons   Each wolf ate ten deer over this period of time.

Fawns born in the spring	+ 150,000
Deer accidentally killed by cars and other vehicles	- 8,000
Deer that died from starvation and other diseases	- 500
Ten wolves died. The remaining 40 adult wolves ate	_____ deer
At the end of this time there were	_____ deer

Fall Season   Each wolf again ate five deer. In fall, the hunting season began.

Deer killed by bow hunters	- 10,000
Deer shot by gun hunters	- 80,000
Deer accidentally killed by cars and other vehicles	- 3,500
Deer that died from starvation and other diseases	- 1,000
Eight of the pups born in spring were still alive. They joined the adult wolves in eating deer. So 48 wolves ate	_____ deer
At the end of the season there were	_____ deer

Go back over the story problem and fill in the blanks.

Number of Deer Killed by **Hunters**	Number of Deer Killed by **Cars**	Number of Deer Killed by **Wolves**	Number of Deer Killed by **Disease, Starvation, and Other Causes**
Winter_____	Winter_____	Winter_____	Winter_____
Spring and Summer_____	Spring and Summer_____	Spring and Summer_____	Spring and Summer_____
Fall_____	Fall_____	Fall_____	Fall_____
Total_____	Total_____	Total_____	Total_____
☐	☐	☐	☐

How are the most deer lost? Number the small boxes in order. Will there be a large number of deer the next year? Should deer hunters worry?

Answers on last page

Studying Wolves

To learn how wolves really live, researchers need to study them in the wild. Scientists look for answers to questions like these:

How large is the wolf's territory?
How much and **what** do they eat?
Are wolves dying? If so, **why**?

Where and **when** do wolves move?
How close do they come to human homes, farms, and towns?

The answers help us understand how much land and food wolves need and how close to humans wolves can live.

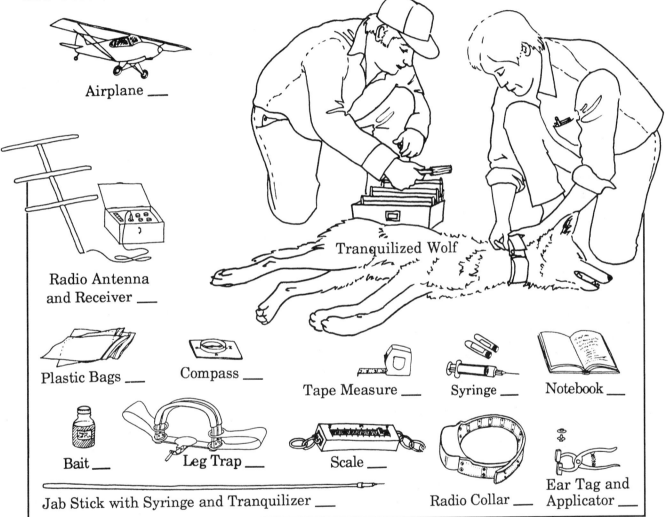

Airplane __

Radio Antenna and Receiver __

Plastic Bags __

Compass __

Tranquilized Wolf

Tape Measure __   Syringe __   Notebook __

Bait __   Leg Trap __   Scale __

Jab Stick with Syringe and Tranquilizer __   Radio Collar __   Ear Tag and Applicator __

Can you match each type of equipment with its correct job?

A. Attracts wolf

B. Catches wolf

C. Shows direction, helping scientist locate wolf

D. Shows wolf's location by sending radio signals from battery-powered transmitter

E. Picks up signal from radio collar—used to locate wolf after release

F. Puts wolf to sleep from a safe distance

G. Weighs wolf

H. Draws blood sample for health tests

I. Measures size of wolf

J. Place to record information

K. Used to collect scat (stool) to study what the wolf is eating

L. Placed on wolf for future identification

M. Used to locate wolves from air

Answers on last page

Tracking Wolves

How do you follow secretive animals in the wilderness when you can't see them? Wolf biologists use **radio tracking**. They can radio-track wolves on foot, from a ground vehicle, an airplane, or even a satellite.

- They capture a wolf, put on a radio collar, and release it.
- Each collar sends out a different radio signal.
- Biologists use a receiver with an antenna to pick up beeping signals from the collar. The signal is the loudest when the antenna is pointed directly at the wolf.

Help the biologists find the wolf pack using radio tracking.
The alpha female is wearing a radio collar. You can locate the pack in two ways:

Method 1

Both biologists are pointing antennas and looking in the direction of the strongest signal. Draw a line from each antenna to the landmark it is pointed at. Circle the spot where the lines cross. You have found the alpha female.

Method 2
(*For Compass Readers*)

The children are giving the reading on their compasses. Draw a line from each compass in the correct direction. Circle where the two lines cross. Again, the wolf is near where the two lines meet. If your two circles are close, you've probably found the alpha wolf and its pack.

This method of finding a wolf from two or more spots, using a compass, is called **triangulation**.

Answer on last page

The Barnyard Mystery

One morning, sheep rancher Anderson discovered a dead sheep in his field. The sheep was surrounded by dog-like footprints. The body had many wounds and was partially eaten.

Mr. Anderson was upset. One of his neighbors jumped to the conclusion that a pack of wolves had killed the sheep and might return to attack his own livestock next. He wanted to destroy all wolves in the area.

Mr. Anderson stopped his neighbor from forming an illegal hunting party to go after the wolves. The rancher explained that "though wolves do occasionally kill livestock, they are also often blamed for livestock killings done by other animals. Let's call in a wildlife control officer to help solve this mystery."

One hour later, a wildlife control officer arrived. First he explained some of the differences between how wolves, dogs, and coyotes hunt.

The Suspects

WOLVES

- are fast, efficient hunters
- leave few signs of trouble
- usually eat or scatter entire **carcass**, body of dead animal, including bones, in a short period of time
- track size 3 to 3-1/2 inches wide by 4 to 4-1/2 inches long

WILD DOGS

- are usually sloppy, inexperienced hunters
- eat little of the carcass
- leave many bites
- tracks may be similar to wolves and coyotes, depending on the size of the breed

COYOTES

- usually grab victim with a bite to the throat or head
- eat part, not all, of carcass, leaving more of skeleton together
- track size 1-3/8 to 2 inches wide by 2-1/2 to 2-3/4 inches long

Next, the control officer looked at the dead sheep and the footprints around it. After an hour, he announced that he knew who had killed the sheep.

Who do you think killed the sheep? What clues in the picture did the wildlife control officer use to solve this case? Use other pages in "Discovering Wolves" to solve the mystery.

Answer on last page

How Could Rancher Anderson Protect His Sheep?

- Buy and train a dog to guard the sheep
- Keep sheep out of the woods
- Remove sick and dying livestock from fields so wolves won't develop a taste for livestock
- Repair broken fences
- Keep pregnant sheep and lambs near the barn

If Wolves Killed The Sheep

Losing a sheep or cow can be a serious problem for ranchers. In some states, ranchers are paid for the cost of sheep or cattle killed by wolves. In states where wolves are "threatened," wildlife control officers can remove and kill wolves that cause problems.

Where Will Wolves

Are wolves gone from most American wild lands forever? Or can they be brought back in some places? The 1973 Endangered Species Act offers some protection for wolves and hope for recovery. The Act makes it illegal to kill, collect, sell, or harm species where they are in danger of becoming extinct. It also requires us to "make room" for endangered and threatened species like the wolf. After studying how and where each animal will best survive, biologists put together **recovery plans.**

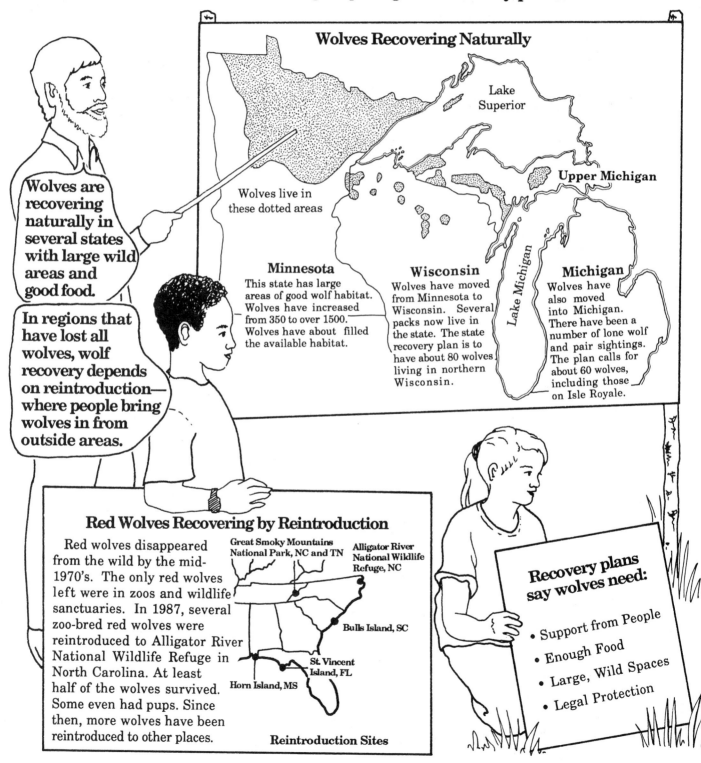

Wolves Recovering Naturally

Lake Superior

Upper Michigan

Lake Michigan

Wolves live in these dotted areas

Wolves are recovering naturally in several states with large wild areas and good food.

In regions that have lost all wolves, wolf recovery depends on reintroduction— where people bring wolves in from outside areas.

Minnesota
This state has large areas of good wolf habitat. Wolves have increased from 350 to over 1500. Wolves have about filled the available habitat.

Wisconsin
Wolves have moved from Minnesota to Wisconsin. Several packs now live in the state. The state recovery plan is to have about 80 wolves living in northern Wisconsin.

Michigan
Wolves have also moved into Michigan. There have been a number of lone wolf and pair sightings. The plan calls for about 60 wolves, including those on Isle Royale.

Red Wolves Recovering by Reintroduction

Red wolves disappeared from the wild by the mid-1970's. The only red wolves left were in zoos and wildlife sanctuaries. In 1987, several zoo-bred red wolves were reintroduced to Alligator River National Wildlife Refuge in North Carolina. At least half of the wolves survived. Some even had pups. Since then, more wolves have been reintroduced to other places.

Great Smoky Mountains National Park, NC and TN

Alligator River National Wildlife Refuge, NC

Bulls Island, SC

St. Vincent Island, FL

Horn Island, MS

Reintroduction Sites

Recovery plans say wolves need:

- Support from People
- Enough Food
- Large, Wild Spaces
- Legal Protection

Howl Tomorrow?

33

Through Indian and Eskimo Eyes

Many Indian and Eskimo groups have had their own special relationship with wolves for centuries. Some of their stories show an understanding of the wolf's place in the world. These stories show respect and admiration for wolves.

Perhaps we are coming closer to their views by watching and studying wolves today.

Eskimos see the wolf and the caribou as one— linked in a special relationship. The caribou feeds the wolf, but the wolf keeps the caribou herd strong—by killing off weak caribou.

Wolf Totem—Some clans, or family groups, of Ojibwe and other tribes use wolves as symbols, or **totems**. Each clan feels a relationship to the animal that is the clan totem. Among other things, Indians admire the wolf's family loyalty, endurance in hunting, and ability to track.

Brother Wolf—People of the Oneida Nation call wolves their brothers. They think it is important to consider and take care of wolves and other creatures in the world.

Wolf Masks—Several tribes of the Pacific Northwest, such as the Quileute, Kwakiutle and Haida, use wolf and other animal masks in ceremonies. Some of these ceremonies welcome young people as full members of a tribe.

Hunting people imitated the wolves ...

by wearing wolf disguises—Indians of the plains, such as the Pawnee and Sioux, used to disguise themselves as wolves. Bison would allow wolves to come close, but they would run away from people.

by cornering prey on ice—Cree and other northern Indians learned from wolves to chase bison onto slippery ice where they were easier to kill.

by attracting prey—The Shoshoni and other western tribes knew antelope would be scared off by a person but not a wolf. The Indian hunter mimicked a wolf lying flat in the prairie grass with only its waving tail visible. The Indian waved a strip of hide until the antelope was within shooting range.

by exhausting prey—Pueblo Indians copied the wolves and ran deer to exhaustion. Relay runners would take turns chasing the deer. Exhausted deer could be killed more easily.

All Species Matter

Wolves share this earth with up to 33 million other animals, plants, and other kinds of life. With all these kinds of living things, does it matter if one, like the wolf, were to become extinct?

Each animal or plant, large or small, has its own special role to play in the way the world works. These plants and animals are all connected and they depend on each other. Often we humans can't see the connections.

Losing a species from the world is like taking a brick out of a house. If you take one away, it weakens the whole. **Color the bricks in the house below.** **Start with number one and color the bricks in order.** Think of each colored brick as a species becoming extinct. How many species can disappear before the house will fall down?

Answer on last page

36

On the Trail of Wolf Words

Across

2. An animal that is hunted and eaten by other animals.
4. A method of putting wolves back into areas where they have disappeared.
6. Sheltered place pups are born.
8. An area a wolf pack defends against other packs.
9. The place an animal, like the wolf, lives and finds food, water, shelter, and space.
11. A group of wolves living together.
12. A wild animal of the dog family.
13. A young wolf.
14. A follower or lower ranking wolf.
15. Odor, often used to mark territory.
16. A wolf that controls or rules a lower ranking wolf is called _____ .

Down

1. Money paid for killing predators, like wolves.
2. An animal that hunts, kills, and eats other animals.
3. Second ranking wolves in pack are called _____ wolves.
5. Living organisms that are in immediate danger of becoming extinct.
7. Biologists follow radio collared wolves by radio _____ .
9. The long, wailing cry of wolves.
10. The top ranking wolves in a pack are the _____ wolves.

Mystery Message

Cross out letters that appear four or more times. Then write the remaining letters in order in the spaces. You will find a mystery message.

BWTIGLNLGYBONUSTPNEGAKGFBOTRWNOGLBVTEGS

_ _ _ _   _ _ _   _ _ _ _ _   _ _ _   _ _ _ _ _ _ ?

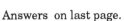
Answers on last page.

What Would You Do If...

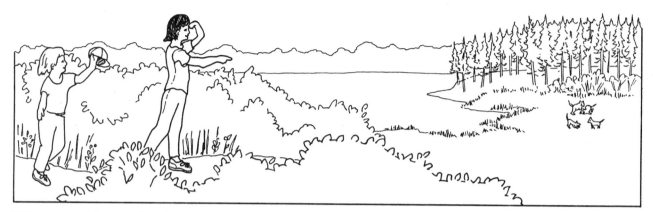

What would you do if you were on a hike and you came upon a group of wolf pups playing at their rendevous site?

_____ A. Get closer for a better view

_____ B. Shout for friends to join you

_____ C. Watch from a distance, briefly, then leave quietly

_____ D. Run away in fear

_____ E. Other _____

What would you do if you were hiking on a trail and you spotted a wolf pack attacking a deer?

_____ A. Watch quietly from a distance

_____ B. Make loud noises to chase the wolves away

_____ C. Leave because you don't want to know what happens

_____ D. Other _____

Answers on last page

What Can I Do?

Wolf Trivia

1. Who would win a broad jump—you or a wolf ?
2. What do wolves do to get cool?
3. How does a wolf help replant the forest in which it lives?
4. How much food can a healthy wolf eat at one feeding? (How many hamburgers would this be for you?)
5. What is the record weight of a wolf ?
6. What is the farthest a wolf pack has traveled in one day?
7. How far has a single wolf ever traveled from its birthplace?
8. What is the "Wolf's Trail to Heaven?"
9. Have wild wolves ever attacked people in North America?

Answers

p. 8   Why Did Wolves Disappear? A. Given; B. Bison and other prey hunted nearly to extinction; C. Illegal hunting; D. Poisoned; E. Shot to protect livestock; F. Habitat loss; Threats Today — C, D, E, and F

p. 15   Family Album: Hierarchy order—There is a male social order and a female social order in each pack, so put the alpha male and female on the top of the ladder followed by beta male, yearlings, and scapegoat

p. 17   How Do Wolves Say Hello? A. I won't fight, I'll obey, B. Hello, C. This is my territory, D. Stay away, E. I won't fight, I'll obey, F. I'm the leader, G. Let's play

p. 18   Calls of the Wild: 1. Howl; 2. Whimper; 3. Growl; 4. Howl, growl, or bark; 5. Whimper; 6. Bark or whimper; 7. Bark or growl; 8. Bark or howl

p. 19   Wolf Talk: There are many possible answers, for example 1. Howling wolves on page 5; 2. Wolves bringing down deer on page 38; 3. Figures F and E on page 17; 4. Wolf scent marking on page 20

p. 20   Keep Off My Property: Twenty cities would fit in pack B's territory. An average size territory is 100 square miles.

p. 24   What's for Dinner? 1. Dall Sheep—escape up cliffs; 2. Caribou—run into open water; 3. Bison—kick or hook with horns; 4. Musk Ox—form defensive circle; 5. Ducks—fly away; 6. White-tailed Deer—run swiftly; 7. Rabbits or Snowshoe Hare in the north—blend with surroundings; 8. Moose—death dealing hoofs; 9. Mice—escape to a safe place; 10. Elk—attack with antlers; 11. Beaver—give warning; 12. Rocky Mountain sheep—gouge with horns

p. 26   Deer Math: 312,610 deer at end of season; Box Order: 1—Hunters, 2—Starvation and disease, 3—Cars, 4 —Wolves.

p. 27   Studying Wolves A. Bait; B. Leg hold trap; C. Compass; D. Radio collar; E. Radio antenna and receiver; F. Jab stick with syringe and tranquilizer; G. Scale; H. Syringe; I. Tape measure; J. Notebook; K. Plastic bags; L. Ear tag; M. Airplane

p. 28   Tracking Wolves: The wolf is 1-1/2 inches above the moose in the water. Do you see its eyes?

p. 30   Barnyard Mystery: The wild dog killed the sheep.

p. 36   All Species Matter: The house would fall down at about brick number 12.

p. 38   In situation 1, C would be a good choice. In situation 2 there is no right answer. It depends on you.

p. 37 Crossword:

```
                B          P R E Y
                O          R
                U          E
      B   RE I N T R O D U C T I O N
DEN       N T   A          T
    T     D Y   T E R R I T O R Y
HAB I TAT A     O          O
O         N     L          PACK
WOLF      G PUP            K
L         E     H          I
    SUBORD I NATE      SCENT
          E          G
      DOM I NANT
```

Mystery Message: Will you speak for wolves?

Trivia Answers. 1. A wolf would win. They can bound 16 feet (5 m) at one try; 2. Pant, flop in creek, hunt at night instead of during the hot day; 3. Seeds of different plants are carried on the wolf's fur. When they drop off miles down the path, they help replant the forest; 4. 20 pounds (9 kg), that would be like you eating 80 hamburgers; 5. 175 pounds (79 kg); 6. 125 miles (201 km) a day was reported by a biologist in Finland; 7. 550 miles (886 km); 8. The Blackfeet Indian's name for the constellation now called the "Milky Way;" 9. There is no record of a healthy, wild wolf killing a person in North America.   * * * * *

Dog-Eared Publications thanks Mark Peterson, wolf biologists Diane Boyd, L. David Mech, Bill Paul, Dick Thiel, Adrian Wydeven, Yellowstone National Park research interpreter Norman A. Bishop, and Ron Refsnider of the U.S. Fish and Wildlife Service Endangered Species Office for technical assistance.

Discovering Wolves was produced in cooperation with the **TIMBER WOLF ALLIANCE**. The **TIMBER WOLF ALLIANCE** was formed to support natural wolf recovery in the Upper Midwest. As a project of the Sigurd Olson Environmental Institute of Northland College in Ashland, Wisconsin, the Alliance develops and distributes educational material about wolves. For information about the Alliance, its Adopt-A-Wolf program, educational materials, products, and a list of other wolf organizations write to: Timber Wolf Alliance, Sigurd Olson Environmental Institute, Northland College, Ashland, Wisconsin 54806-3999